THE SEVEN WONDERS
OF THE MODERN WORLD

THE COLOSSEUM

BY ELIZABETH NOLL

BELLWETHER MEDIA • MINNEAPOLIS, MN

BLASTOFF!
DISCOVERY

Blastoff! Discovery launches a new mission: reading to learn. Filled with facts and features, each book offers you an exciting new world to explore!

BLASTOFF! UNIVERSE

BLASTOFF! Beginners — GRADE K

BLASTOFF! READERS — GRADES 1-3

BLASTOFF! DISCOVERY — GRADE 4

This edition first published in 2021 by Bellwether Media, Inc.

No part of this publication may be reproduced in whole or in part without written permission of the publisher.
For information regarding permission, write to Bellwether Media, Inc., Attention: Permissions Department, 6012 Blue Circle Drive, Minnetonka, MN 55343.

Library of Congress Cataloging-in-Publication Data

Names: Noll, Elizabeth, author.
Title: The Colosseum / by Elizabeth Noll.
Description: Minneapolis, MN : Bellwether Media, 2021 | Series: The Seven Wonders of the Modern World | Includes bibliographical references and index. | Audience: Ages 7-13 | Audience: Grades 4-6 | Summary: "Engaging images accompany information about the Colosseum. The combination of high-interest subject matter and narrative text is intended for students in grades 3 through 8"–Provided by publisher.
Identifiers: LCCN 2020018904 (print) | LCCN 2020018905 (ebook) | ISBN 9781644872673 (library binding) | ISBN 9781681037301 (ebook)
Subjects: LCSH: Colosseum (Rome, Italy)–Juvenile literature. | Amphitheaters–Rome–Juvenile literature. | Rome (Italy)–Buildings, structures, etc.–Juvenile literature. | Architecture, Roman–Italy–Rome–Juvenile literature.
Classification: LCC DG68.1 .N65 2021 (print) | LCC DG68.1 (ebook) | DDC 937/.63–dc23
LC record available at https://lccn.loc.gov/2020018904
LC ebook record available at https://lccn.loc.gov/2020018905

Text copyright © 2021 by Bellwether Media, Inc. BLASTOFF! DISCOVERY and associated logos are trademarks and/or registered trademarks of Bellwether Media, Inc.

Editor: Betsy Rathburn   Designer: Brittany McIntosh

Printed in the United States of America, North Mankato, MN.

TABLE OF CONTENTS

Welcome to Rome! You step off of a train at Termini Station. Dozens of train tracks lead in every direction. Italy's busy capital city bustles around you. You make your way through the crowd, eager to see the sights. Where will you go first?

Rome is full of history! Other ancient structures in the city include the Roman Forum, the Pantheon, and the Arch of Constantine!

Your map tells you that historic sites are nearby. Another quick train ride brings you steps away from the Colosseum. You enter the ancient stadium and climb to the top for a 360-degree view of the city. Ancient history and modern Italy come together at the Colosseum!

THE HEART OF AN EMPIRE

The Colosseum is a world-famous **amphitheater** in Rome, Italy. Rome is on the banks of the Tiber River. Around 2,000 years ago, this city was the center of a huge empire. The Colosseum showed off the empire's wealth and power. It still stands as a **symbol** of Rome today!

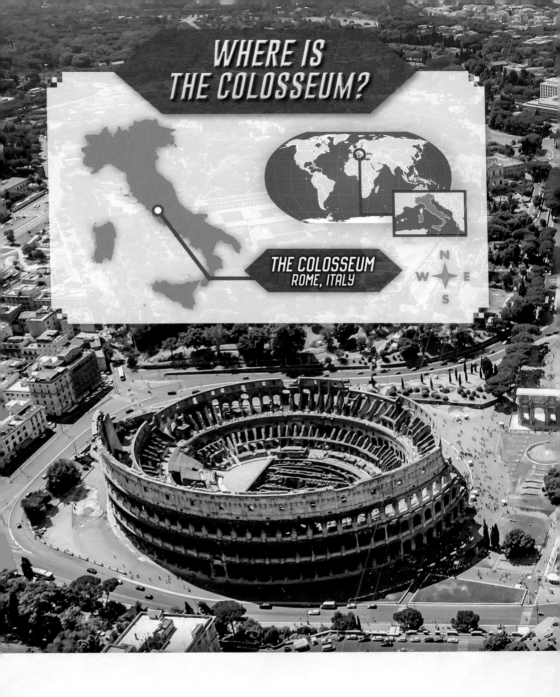

WHERE IS THE COLOSSEUM?

THE COLOSSEUM
ROME, ITALY

N W E S

The stadium stands more than 150 feet (46 meters) tall. Its original name was the Flavian Amphitheater. About 50,000 people could fit inside!

THINK ABOUT IT

Why do you think the builders made the Colosseum so big?

COLUMN

The Colosseum is an oval-shaped building made of limestone, concrete, and brick. One side of the structure has four stories of **arches** and columns. Small windows on the top story show small sections of sky. On the other side of the Colosseum, the upper levels have crumbled away over many centuries.

Inside, several tiers look down over the center of the Colosseum. Over time, the central floor has worn away. Visitors can see down into the lower level. The many windows look out over the busy city.

ARCHES AND EMPERORS

Around the year 70 CE, Emperor Vespasian ordered work on the Colosseum. He wanted to show the importance of the Roman Empire. He also wanted to keep Romans happy. The previous emperor was cruel. Vespasian knew that building an amphitheater would make himself popular.

It took builders two years just to make the Colosseum's **foundation**. They wanted to make sure the huge building would not sink or tilt. They dug out a huge hole and filled it with concrete. Seven years later, the building was still only finished to the third story.

ANCIENT ROME

QUARRY IN TIVOLI, ITALY

Building the Colosseum took a lot of effort. More than 50,000 people worked on the structure. Many of the workers were **slaves**. They brought building materials in from **quarries** many miles from Rome. A new road was built to make transport easier. Every day, wagons traveled down the road to pick up new loads of stone.

Work was not over when the stones arrived in Rome. They needed to be carved into the right shape. Then, wooden cranes lifted the heavy pieces into position. Special Roman cement held the rocks in place.

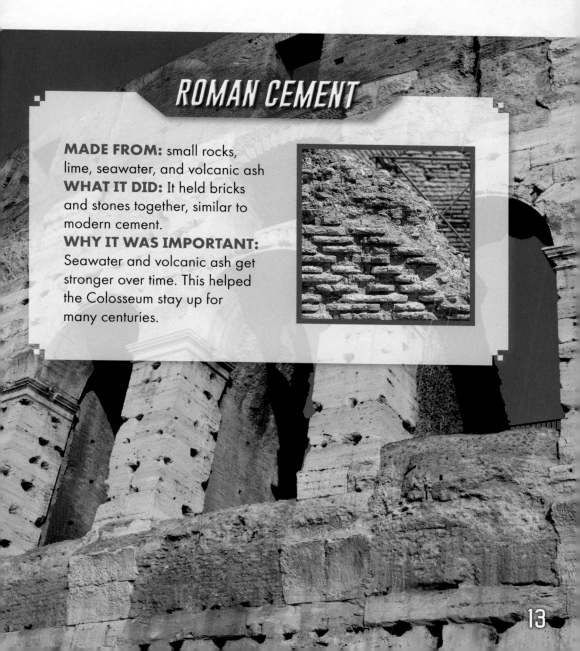

ROMAN CEMENT

MADE FROM: small rocks, lime, seawater, and volcanic ash
WHAT IT DID: It held bricks and stones together, similar to modern cement.
WHY IT WAS IMPORTANT: Seawater and volcanic ash get stronger over time. This helped the Colosseum stay up for many centuries.

THEN AND NOW

THEN

Wooden cranes used human power to lift heavy objects with ropes. People walked in a large wheel. When the wheel turned, the ropes lifted.

NOW

Metal cranes powered by fuel engines lift heavy objects. An operator uses buttons and levers to control the machine. Structures are built much faster!

KEYSTONE

The builders used arches to make the Colosseum stronger. Stones were stacked on top of columns in a rounded shape. Then they were held in place with central **keystones**. These helped the arches support themselves. They could also support heavy loads from upper levels. This helped workers build the Colosseum to four stories.

When the four stories were complete, the Colosseum was ready for a top! Several **awnings** were made out of huge pieces of cloth. The awnings protected people from sun and rain. They could be opened and closed to let air flow!

AWNING

It took many years to complete the Colosseum. Vespasian died in 79, the year before the stadium opened. His son Titus became the next emperor. Emperor Titus held events to celebrate the grand opening. The contests were very violent. **Gladiators** fought to the death. They also hunted wild animals such as elephants, lions, and tigers. In 100 days, more than 9,000 animals and about 2,000 people were killed.

GLADIATOR

BOAT BATTLES

Titus was the first emperor to hold naval battles at the Colosseum. The stadium was flooded with water, and gladiators fought aboard boats!

Most gladiators were prisoners of war, criminals, or slaves. They trained at gladiator schools and learned to use weapons. Their fighting skills entertained thousands of Romans.

HYPOGEUM

After only a short time as emperor, Titus died. His younger brother, Domitian, became emperor. Domitian continued construction on the Colosseum. He completed the top story. He also ordered prisoners to make passages underneath the arena. This underground area was called the *hypogeum*. It held cages that carried animals and gladiators up to trap doors in the floor of the Colosseum.

The hypogeum made contests even more popular.
Gladiators and animals seemed to appear on the arena floor
out of nowhere. Spectators loved these surprising matches!

THE END OF THE FIGHTS

Over the centuries, Christianity spread throughout the Roman Empire. This changed many people's feelings about the gladiator fights. In 325, Emperor Constantine tried to stop the fights. But he was not successful. A few years later, Constantine moved the capital to modern-day Turkey. Constantinople became the new center of the empire.

After this, Rome's population slowly declined. There was not enough money for the costly fights. But the contests continued on a smaller scale. In 404, Emperor Honorius banned gladiator fights. But prisoners still hunted wild animals for another 100 years. The last known fight was held in 523.

CONSTANTINOPLE

THINK ABOUT IT

Why did moving the capital make Rome's population decline?

ANIMAL BATTLE AT THE COLOSSEUM

21

Some structures built with stone from the Colosseum still stand today! One is the Palace of St. Mark, built in the 1400s!

After the battles ended, people used the Colosseum for many different things. A **chapel** and a cemetery were built there. People also built houses, workshops, and gardens inside the Colosseum's walls. The amphitheater became almost like a village. Around 1200 CE, a wealthy family moved in and used it as their castle.

Over the centuries, earthquakes shook the Colosseum. An earthquake in 1349 brought down the walls on the south side. Some people took stones that had fallen and used them for their own houses. **Popes** and city leaders took cartloads of stone from the Colosseum to build and repair palaces, churches, and other buildings!

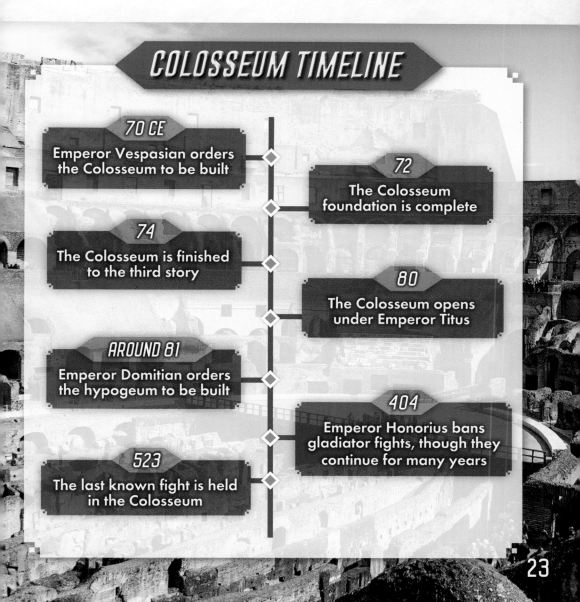

COLOSSEUM TIMELINE

70 CE
Emperor Vespasian orders the Colosseum to be built

72
The Colosseum foundation is complete

74
The Colosseum is finished to the third story

80
The Colosseum opens under Emperor Titus

AROUND 81
Emperor Domitian orders the hypogeum to be built

404
Emperor Honorius bans gladiator fights, though they continue for many years

523
The last known fight is held in the Colosseum

By the 1800s, the Colosseum was popular with travelers. Artists and writers visited to admire the building's beauty. Scientists arrived to study the Colosseum. **Botanists** counted over 400 different kinds of plants at the Colosseum. Some did not grow anywhere else in Europe! The seeds were likely carried on the fur of wild animals from other continents.

TIME TO MOW

Scientists found more than 50 types of grass growing in the Colosseum!

MARBLE STATUES

Soon, Italian **archaeologists** rediscovered details of the building's past. They dug down into the floor and discovered the hypogeum. They found animal and human bones. They also found pipes and pieces of marble statues. These discoveries helped researchers begin to understand how ancient Romans used the Colosseum!

25

A MODERN WONDER

Today the Colosseum is one of the world's most popular **tourist** attractions. It was named a Wonder of the Modern World in 2007. In 2018, more than 7 million people visited the ruin! People visit the Colosseum to learn about ancient Rome. Visitors can look at sculptures and other **artifacts** that archaeologists have **excavated**.

People visit for special events, too. Every Easter, the Pope performs a Catholic ceremony there. Many famous musicians have also performed inside the Colosseum's ancient walls!

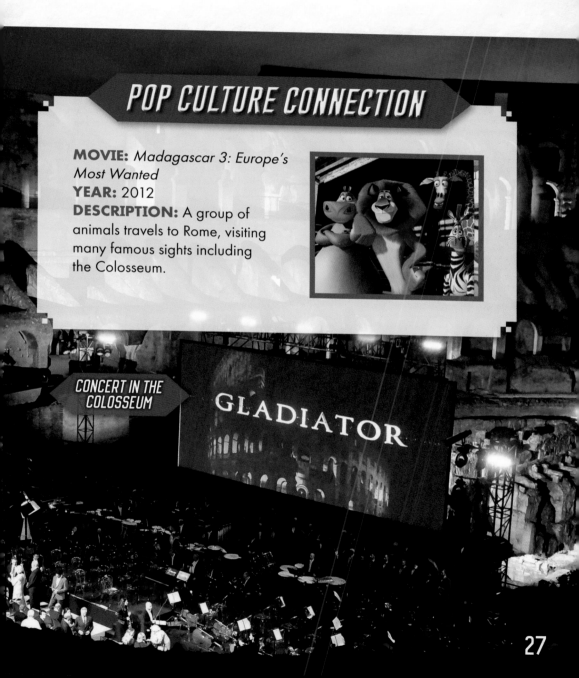

POP CULTURE CONNECTION

MOVIE: *Madagascar 3: Europe's Most Wanted*
YEAR: 2012
DESCRIPTION: A group of animals travels to Rome, visiting many famous sights including the Colosseum.

CONCERT IN THE COLOSSEUM

GLADIATOR

Some people are working to repair and **restore** the Colosseum. In 2012, an Italian businessman pledged to spend millions of dollars to restore the building. One major project was having the walls cleaned. The workers did not use chemicals. They used only water, so that they would not damage the stones. In 2015, the Italian government promised to spend $20 million to rebuild the ancient arena's floor.

RESTORATION

COMPARE AND CONTRAST

THE COLOSSEUM

THE SUPERDOME

LOCATION
Rome, Italy

HEIGHT
more than 150 feet
(46 meters) tall

YEARS BUILT
between 70 and 80 CE

MATERIALS
limestone, concrete, brick

SEATING CAPACITY
about 50,000

USES
gladiator games, animal battles

LOCATION
New Orleans, Louisiana

HEIGHT
273 feet
(83 meters) tall

YEARS BUILT
between 1971 and 1975

MATERIALS
steel

SEATING CAPACITY
about 75,000

USES
sporting events, concerts,
emergency shelter

In 2017, the top two floors of the Colosseum were opened to tourists for the first time in decades. Also that year, there was an **exhibit** that explained the building's history to visitors. There is much to discover at Rome's ancient Colosseum!

29

GLOSSARY

amphitheater–a building used for special events

archaeologists–scientists who study things left behind by ancient people

arches–curved structures that provide support

artifacts–items made long ago by humans; artifacts tell people today about people from the past.

awnings–rooflike covers often made out of fabric

botanists–people who study plant life

chapel–a small building where religious worship happens

excavated–dug out and removed

exhibit–a display

foundation–a base or support on top of which a structure is built

gladiators–people who fought to the death to provide entertainment

keystones–wedge-shaped pieces at the tops of arches that hold other pieces in place

popes–the heads of the Roman Catholic Church

quarries–places from which rocks are dug for use in building

restore–to return something to its original condition

slaves–people who do work for another person without pay

symbol–something that stands for something else

tourist–related to people who travel to visit a place

TO LEARN MORE

AT THE LIBRARY

Oachs, Emily Rose. *Ancient Rome*. Minneapolis, Minn.: Bellwether Media, 2020.

O'Connor, Jim. *Where Is the Colosseum?* New York, N.Y.: Grosset & Dunlap, 2017.

Rechner, Amy. *Italy*. Minneapolis, Minn.: Bellwether Media, 2018.

ON THE WEB

FACTSURFER

Factsurfer.com gives you a safe, fun way to find more information.

1. Go to www.factsurfer.com.

2. Enter "Colosseum" into the search box and click 🔍.

3. Select your book cover to see a list of related content.

INDEX